THE SACRAMENT OF REPENTANCE AND CONFESSION

Individual Guide

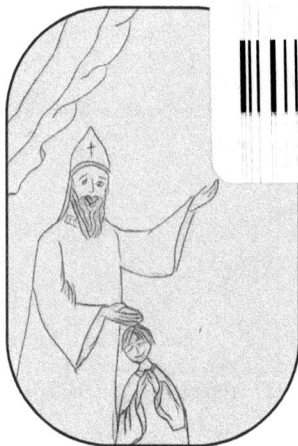

By Kristin Sarkis Youssef
and under the supervision of
Fr. Mina Salama

THE PARTHENOS PRESS

Contents

Preface

The purpose of the Church's spiritual life emphasized in the liturgical prayers and all its sacraments is the return of the believers to God and establishing a fellowship with the Holy Trinity.

A great emphasis is placed on four of the seven sacraments of the Church as they are deemed essential for our salvation. These four sacraments are: Baptism, Chrismation, Repentance and Confession, and the Eucharist.

In this short guide, Mrs. Kiristin Sarkis Youssef has compiled together a confession guide that is extremely easy to read and follow. The goal of this guide is to help understand the importance of the Sacrament of Repentance and Confession while alleviating many of the popular questions and myths that many have surrounding the Sacrament.

May God bless this work for the glory of His Holy Name and reward the writer with the heavenly rewards and may it bring forth the desired spiritual fruit through the blessings and prayers of H.H. Pope Tawadros II, Amen.

Fr. Mina Salama
St. Mary's Coptic Orthodox Church (Lynnwood, WA)

Introduction

"I say to you that likewise there will be more joy in heaven over one sinner who repents than over ninety-nine just persons who need no repentance" (Luke 15:7).

Confession is when one meets with the Lord Jesus Christ in the presence of the priest to reconcile with God, offer repentance, declare one's love for Him, and end one's isolation from God [caused by one's sin].

Repentance comes from the Greek word μετάνοια [*metanoia*], and it means to have a change [*meta*] of mind/ heart [*noia*].

"There is no sin that cannot be forgiven except the one without repentance." – St. Isaac the Syrian

Before Confession

Before Confession is Repentance!

Repentance is a change of mind that results in a change of action. St. Paul teaches us, saying, "but declared first to those in Damascus and in Jerusalem, and throughout all the region of Judea, and then to the Gentiles, that they should repent, turn to God, and do works befitting repentance" (Acts 26:20).

Repentance can often be mistaken for feelings of guilt or remorse. It is important to know that these feelings are a sign of true repentance, but not repentance itself. The full biblical definition of repentance is change in mind and action.

Use the following guide to help you prepare for confession and practice repentance.

- Stand in silence for a few minutes before God in prayer asking for guidance from the Holy Spirit.

- Using the guide provided below spend some time reflecting on obstacles that prevent you from having a close relationship with God; self-reflect and examine your relationships with God, self and people.

- Offer repentance by identifying specific areas in your life where you would like to implement change.

- Pray the Agpeya's Repentance and Before Confession prayer.

Repentance Prayer [1]

My Lord, God and Savior Jesus Christ, treasure of mercy and spring of salvation, I come to You confessing my sins. I confess that with boldness I dared to defile Your holy sanctuary with my sins. Now I seek Your mercy and love, for Your mercies are boundless; You never turn back a sinner who comes to You. I confess to You. I confess that my mind is burdened with sin and that I have no strength left. Do not turn away from me; do not rebuke me in Your anger nor chasten me in Your displeasure. I am worn out; have compassion upon me, O Lord. Do not judge me according to Your justice, but according to Your mercy. Remember Your creation; do not put me on trial, because none of Your servants can justify their deeds. Dress me in a new attire that befits Your glory. Forgive my sins and I shall sing, "Blessed is he whose sins are forgiven." When I confess my sins and reveal my iniquities, You cleanse me. Amen.

✢✢✢

Use the following guide to help you self-reflect and examine your relationships with God, self and people, before you meet your spiritual father for confession.

Relationship with God[2]

Lack of prayer, mediation, bible reading, and communion, not paying tithes, saying the Lord's name in vain, not honoring the poor, the widow, and the needy, lack of fasting, service, spiritual reading, and participating in church services, stealing the glory of God, complaining, blaming God, lack of reverence in the presence of God, not doing good deeds (love, giving, caring, forgiving, helping, etc.), not fulfilling the commandments of God, doubting His promises, distractions in prayer, not respecting the house of God, unthankfulness, fear, etc.

Relationship with Self[2]

Hopelessness, despair, pride, smoking, drinking alcohol, addictions, gambling, comparing myself to others, unreasonable use of video games, social media, and phones, holding grudges, listening to worldly music, gluttony, wasting time, stealing the glory of God, pornography, lustful sins, listening to rumors, gossip, judgment of others, and inappropriate conversations, love of praise, impatience, laziness, carelessness, self-excuses, self-pity, entitlement, lack of compassion, self-righteousness, stubbornness, negligence, bad intensions, attachment to the world, etc.

Relationship with People[2]

Anger, contention, lustful relationships, insults, bad company, bullying, aggressiveness, pride, violence, hardness, hypocrisy, cheating, injustice, being a stumbling block, adultery, love of praise, wishing evil for others, gossiping, rejoicing in evil, lying, foolish conversation, bad words, swearing, disclosing secrets, showing off, bad jokes, wearing revealing clothes, stealing, hatred, abusive behavior, disobedience (specially to parents), not fulfilling promises, selfishness, envy, jealousy, blaming others, being embarrassed of family members, bad intensions, spreading negativity, bad attitude, lack of respect to others (specially elders), rudeness, etc.

✤✤✤

Prayer Before Confession[3]

My Holy Father, who delights in the repentance of sinners, You promised that You are ready to accept them. Look now, my Lord, upon a sinning soul which went astray in valleys of rebellion for a long time, in which it was embittered and felt its misery, estranged from the fountain of its salvation. Now I proceed to You asking You for its purification from the filthiness and mud in which it was wallowing. Accept it and do not reject it, for if You look at it in Your kindness and deal with it in Your tender mercy, it will be purified and saved, and if You ignore it, it will perish and fall into perdition. Grant me, O Lord, a grace by which I dare approach You with strong faith and complete and perfect hope in order to confess my iniquities and hate to return to them. Let Your Spirit rebuke me for my sins. Enlighten my heart to recognize how much I have sinned, transgressed, missed, and broken Your commandments, and how many times I failed to do those things You would have me do. Grant me, O Lord, to determine not to return to sin in order to dwell in You and keep Your commandments so that I may live for glorifying You Holy Name. Amen.

During Confession

Repentance is complete when followed by confession.

"The moments of confession are moments at the feet of the Crucified, where you and the priest would enjoy His wondrous work." – Fr. Tadros Malaty[4]

During confession you are speaking with Christ in the presence of the priest. Some people vocalize this understanding, stating, "absolve me father, for I have sinned against my Lord Jesus Christ."

Use the following guide during confession.

- Start with the heaviest sin first, so you can clear your mind for the rest of confession.

- Do not hide or be ashamed to confess any sin, but do not give many details regarding the sins.

- Do not focus guidance time on the past but rather on the future. Sins, of which you have already repented and which you have confessed to God and the priest, are forgiven.

- Make sure you seek spiritual canon from the priest during confession, and make note of it!

After Confession

- Thank God for His mercy and forgiveness, and ask Him to restore His Image in you so you live guided by the Spirit, and be an image of Christ, your Creator.
- Make a commitment to not fall back into old habits and ask God to help you fulfill your heart's desire to overcome old habits and sinful ways.
- Write down the advice your spiritual father gives you, especially your spiritual cannon.
- Pray the Agpeya's After Confession prayer.

✤✤✤

Prayer After Confession[3]

I thank Your goodness, O Father, the Lover of Mankind, for You did not wish that I should perish, but You wakened me from my forgetfulness, guided me into Your way, and restored me from the valley of perdition into the refuge of Your safe fortress. Fill me with hope and faith. I proceeded unto You, O Lord, like a patient who comes to the healing physician, and like the hungry to life-sustaining food, and like the thirsty to the springs of living water, and like the poor to the source of richness, and like the sinner to the Savior, and like the dead to the fountain of life. You are my salvation, my physician, my strength, my comfort, and my happiness. In You is my rest, so help me and guard me. Encompass me and teach me to put all my will in Your hands and walk according to what you wish. Help my weakness that I may dwell and be steadfast and continue to be faithful to You unto the end. Amen.

Frequently Asked Questions

- **Why repentance and confession? I do not want to stop; I am not hurting anyone.**

Christ teaches us to "repent for the Kingdom of God is at hand" (Matthew 4:17), and tells us "… but unless you repent you will all likewise perish" (Luke 13:3).

There is a constant need to be reconciled with God to come back to oneself, and we do that through repentance and confession.

- **Why go to the priest? Is repentance not enough? Can I just confess to God?**

Scriptures teach us about repentance and confession and invite us to practice them both simultaneously; for one does not take part without the other. For example, when the Lord spoke to Saul on his way to Damascus, trembling and astonished Saul asked the Lord what He wants him to do; and the Lord said to him, "Arise and go into the city, and you will be told what you must do" (Acts 9:6). Saul then met with Ananias, repented, confessed, was baptized and was healed when Ananias laid his hands on him, asking the Lord that Saul may receive his sight back and be filled with the Holy Spirit (Acts 9:17).

- **I confess my sins but keep repeating them; what's the point of confession?**

Do not be discouraged when you fall into temptation; rise

up and ask the Lord to be light to you as you continue your fight against evil.

Trace your steps and find how/where you have fallen, repent, and confess to the priest.

- **Do priests share people's confession with other people?**

No! Confession is confidential and it is between you, God, and the priest. All priesthood ranks in the Church are not allowed to share a person's confession under any circumstances without the person's consent.

Priests themselves have fathers of confessions.

- **I do not know what to say in confession; it is too embarrassing!!**

Spiritual fathers in the Church are guided by the Holy Spirit to help people with many spiritual life challenges, including confession. Have an honest conversation with your spiritual father and tell him exactly how you feel openly and honestly.

Confession helps us overcome pride, and maintains the spirit of discipleship in the one apostolic Church.

References

[1] *Agpeya: Prayer Book of the Hours.* (Sandia, TX: St. Mary and St. Moses Abbey Press, 2018).

[2] Dimitri, Fr. Mina, *What to Say in Confession?* (East Brunswick, NJ: St. Mary Coptic Orthodox Church).

[3] *The Agpeya: The Coptic Prayer Book of the Seven Hours,* Azmy, Fr. Abraham Ed. (Hamden, CT: St. Virgin Mary and Archangel Michael Coptic Orthodox Church of Connecticut, 2009).

[4] Malaty, Fr. Tadros. *Al-Tawbah Wa Al-Ih'tiraf* [Repentance and Confession]. (Egypt: St. Mina the Wonder Worker Monastery in Mariuot).

NOTES

www.ingramcontent.com/pod-product-compliance
Lightning Source LLC
Chambersburg PA
CBHW021124020426
42331CB00004B/619